IN REVERIE

BETH

Presentation by BookLeaf Publishing

Web: www.bookleafpub.com

E-mail: info@bookleafpub.com

ISBN: 9789358363173

First edition 2021

To all the souls who mirror my own.

ACKNOWLEDGEMENT

To whom I was six years ago, thank you.
Thank you for hurting, yet refusing to give up on love.
Even when it was the sole thing you were convinced that broke you.

One.

in dreaming wake I meet your soul
when time is still and reality untouched.
in the fantastical play of a higher
dimension,
we dance like the night
and breathe fire to the heavens.
hush,
twirl,
catch honey from my lips.
take flight across the divide
and bind us infinitely in gold.
our souls alight,
watch them cascade in bloom,
and into petals of love
may they bless the lonely with hope.
for when eyelids are rested
and heartbeats find calm,
trust the echoes that guide us
as the callings of our flame.

Two.

please sing me a lullaby
with the musings of your dreams.
do show me the sunset
through the glow of a hopeful heart.
in the silence of temptation
and the flickering of desire,
teach me the origins of romance
with the grace of lovers past.
could you whisper the words of April
to paint colour with the hues of May?
so when June falls to slumber
and the moon is basking high,
would you bathe me in the starlight until
the daffodils break bloom?
surrender to the evening
and let time hold us dear,
for until the aurora's rising
we have each other to keep in light.

Three.

and in that moment she knew,
why the world had fallen to ash when
only yesterday felt like daybreak.
why parents had blackened sunsets and
turned marigolds into mulch.
she knew why neighbours cursed the
rain
and why the wicked taunted the poor.
she knew why scholars mocked the
poets
and why lions made lunch of the lame.
in that moment she knew,
and felt grateful to have known.
because to know tragedy was to know
heartbreak,
and to know heartbreak was to feel joy.
to feel joy was to remember serenity,
and to remember serenity was to find
peace.
so in that moment she knew,
that the world was vicious and
unforgiving,
and thus - in its right - was kind
and ready to begin anew.

Four.

in the wake of destruction lies the breath
of a new beginning,
amongst ashes of flaming ruin live the
embers of rising glow.
tell me - do you see
within the bruising of her soul,
the hope of a childhood dream
which longs to one day burst forth.
do you feel her warmth and grace
in the way she loves the lonely?
can you sense her deepest dreams
when she gazes at the moon?
through tears and timid smiles
can you know how much she cares,
and how little she feels she's worth from
those who fail to love her.
be gentle with her heart
for its pain could echo the seas,
but to love her is to live her
and what a spectacular life to breathe.

Five.

love her wild as nature intended,
let her roam with the galaxies in flight.
do carry her soul,
but may her footsteps make marks
with the glow of her fire in the path she
forges free.
untamed is her heart
and ferociously does she live
for, to her, the challenge awaits
and the gauntlet cries her name.
hear her bellow the call of the titans and
conquer the waves of the sea,
she is all to be marvelled
so love her deeply,
love her free.

Six.

to my lover,
my dearest one,
look for me in the dawn of the day.
in the breaking of light that brings wake
to the birdsong.
feel my breath in the gossamer, fall-time
breeze
and linger in lust with the spirits of gale.
in the glow of the moon
and the shadow of the sun,
make it known that I see you
in every beauty of life.
and hold me dear
in the warmth of your soul,
with the tenderest care
and the most eternal of light.

Seven.

her spirit was the wind
taming the wildest of souls,
on the shoulders of the free
she summoned silver to fall in glow.
uninhibited
and without shame,
watch her burst from the roots of
uncertainty.
and in the glory of her expansion,
feel her worth
and the presence of power.

Eight.

you remind me of that Summer,
by the sea tide in the bay.
when the daylight made me freckle
and each moment was tinted in gold.
back to child's play
and lolly bags,
to the sweetness of each hour.
when time gave breath to the morrow
and lit the lamp posts after dark.
you remind me of the good,
of the sparkling, waking dawn
and to hold you in my heart
is to live eternally in its glow.

Nine.

if time was a friend, perhaps our names
would be lovers,
our fingers like thread
woven delicate and clean.
if circumstance was kinder, would our
eyes be our mirrors?
gazing deep into a soul
that has longed to see its own.
if choices were made,
and words not unsaid,
would you live by my side as the solace
to the storm?
may we rival the greatest oceans
and lay waste to the gardens of Rome,
for our love would be cataclysmic
for all of history and her affairs.

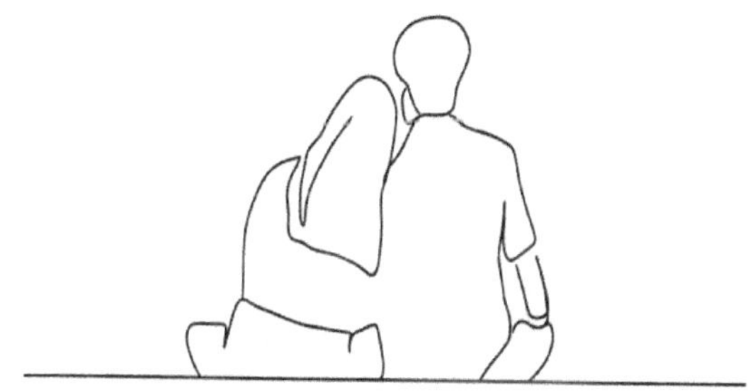

Ten.

tell me
a truth only souls can know,
in whispered words from an unspoken
heart.
spell it deeply with your eyes,
trace it slowly with your voice,
speak it lovingly with your gaze,
and sing it wildly with your touch.
listen to these musings to uncover me
fully.
my greatest depths are yours to learn
and lay bare.
but only through the language that
reality cannot fathom,
only through each other,
between the embers of a kin.

Eleven.

one day, I will find it
the love of which I dream.
I know it – I believe it,
the love of which I'm worthy.
for my struggles to have purpose,
not my tears to fall in vain,
that the breakings of my heart are the
rebirths of my soul.
one day, it will be real.
one day, it will be love.
and the shattered mosaic within me will
gleam in its euphoria.

Twelve.

do you know what I see when I look into
your eyes?
it's home, it's heart, it's hope.
when the days are long and the nights
too cold,
it's calm, it's warmth, it's bliss.
dreaming wake is a genial truth,
and rose-tinted memories are my very
own thoughts.
to love with you
is to revel in fantasy,
that beckons to sing freely amongst the
melancholy of tomorrow.
so let it, I say,
let it dance, let it free.
for with you, I see colour,
 amidst a worldly tint of grey.

Thirteen.
I dreamt of who, and what, and when.
I dreamt of kisses, and lips, and
laughter.
I saw his face – but it was blurred.
I heard his voice – yet it was mute.
you were there – yet out of reach,
and I could feel you,
I could love you.

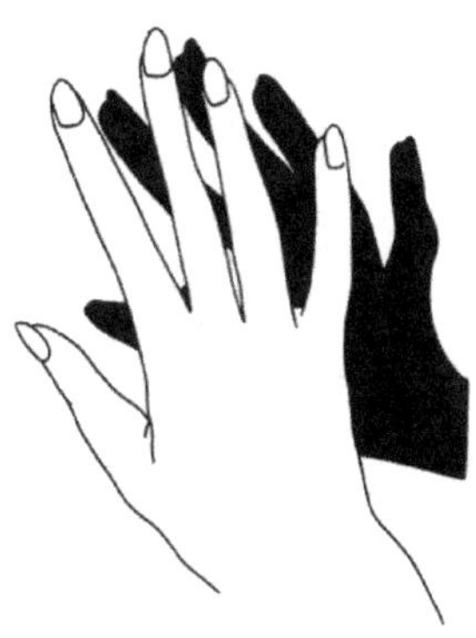

Fourteen.

do you dream of me in refuge,
do you think of us in moonlight?
do hearts echo the weight of absence,
and miss the space I fill in Love?
tell me, if you do,
if you long for soul connection.
for if Time was but folly,
and Distance a mere sundry,
I would lay with you forever,
and one day more, after that.

Fifteen.
so love is dangerous, they say,
one sip enough to drown.
then pour me seven glasses,
and watch me die in liquid ecstasy.

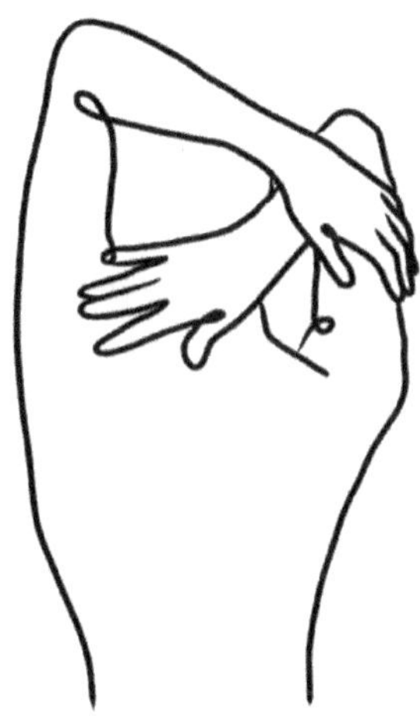